IT'S TIME TO LEARN ABOUT CRABS

It's Time to Learn about Crabs

Walter the Educator

Silent King Books
A WhichHead Entertainment Imprint

Copyright © 2025 by Walter the Educator

All rights reserved. No part of this book may be reproduced in any manner whatsoever without written per- mission except in the case of brief quotations embodied in critical articles and reviews.

First Printing, 2024

Disclaimer

This book is a literary work; the story is not about specific persons, locations, situations, and/or circumstances unless mentioned in a historical context. Any resemblance to real persons, locations, situations, and/or circumstances is coincidental. This book is for entertainment and informational purposes only. The author and publisher offer this information without warranties expressed or implied. No matter the grounds, neither the author nor the publisher will be accountable for any losses, injuries, or other damages caused by the reader's use of this book. The use of this book acknowledges an understanding and acceptance of this disclaimer.

It's Time to Learn about Crabs is a collectible early learning book by Walter the Educator suitable for all ages belonging to Walter the Educator's Time to Eat Book Series. Collect more books at WaltertheEducator.com

USE THE EXTRA SPACE TO TAKE NOTES AND DOCUMENT YOUR MEMORIES

CRABS

Let's take a walk along the sand,

It's Time to Learn about

Crabs

Where little crabs dig in the land.

They scurry sideways, never still,

With legs that move with crabby skill.

Crabs are animals, yes it's true,

But they're not quite like me or you.

They don't have fur or feathers bright

They wear hard shells, a sturdy sight!

These creatures live near sea and shore,

And sometimes in the ocean floor.

They're part of a group with a long, cool name

Say "crustaceans," that's their fame!

Crustaceans have a shell outside,

To keep them safe, a place to hide.

It's called an exoskeleton,

Their armor shining in the sun.

It's Time to Learn about

Crabs

They have jointed legs, not just one pair

Ten legs total, walking everywhere!

Two of those legs are big and strong,

They're called claws, and they help all day long.

Crabs use their claws to fight and eat,

To break up shells or grab a treat.

They munch on seaweed, fish, or sand,

Whatever food they find near land.

Some crabs dig holes or hide in rocks,

Some drift with seaweed, like floating docks.

They might be tiny or quite wide

So many crab types live worldwide!

They breathe through gills, like fish, you see,

But they can walk on land like you and me.

That's why they scuttle on the shore,

It's Time to Learn about

Crabs

Then splash back to the sea once more.

Hermit crabs don't grow a shell,

So they find one that fits them well.

When they grow big, they swap it out

A perfect fit, there is no doubt!

So now you know just what they are

Crustaceans with a shell like a car!

If you see a crab, give a wave hello,

It's Time to Learn about

Crabs

They're clever and cool, wherever they go!

ABOUT THE CREATOR

Walter the Educator is one of the pseudonyms for Walter Anderson. Formally educated in Chemistry, Business, and Education, he is an educator, an author, a diverse entrepreneur, and he is the son of a disabled war veteran. "Walter the Educator" shares his time between educating and creating. He holds interests and owns several creative projects that entertain, enlighten, enhance, and educate, hoping to inspire and motivate you. Follow, find new works, and stay up to date with Walter the Educator™

at WaltertheEducator.com

www.ingramcontent.com/pod-product-compliance
Lightning Source LLC
LaVergne TN
LVHW051920060526
838201LV00060B/4100